I0447935

Acknowledgements

For all the cool colorists across the world who encouraged me to keep on drawing and bringing you yet another book. Thank you so much for your love and encouragement.

Thanks to my brilliant colorist team who are also motivators for me, Debbie West Cumming, Dee Dee Boseman, Elisabeth Anderson, Margolet Van Zyl, Marley Morris, Michelle A. Turner, Tamara Slaten.

Special thanks to Dee Dee Boseman, Naomi McClelland, Cindy Nation, Jody Anne Savage and Jade Elizabeth for their awesome advises and ideas.

IMPORTANT INFORMATION FOR USING THIS BOOK

• This book contains 50 hand-drawn plus digitally illustrations to color, each is printed **SINGLE SIDED** (back is blank). 36 pages from edition 1 plus bonus pages making total of 50 designs!

• The pages are printed on #60 lb bright white paper which performs well for all brands of colored pencils and crayons, without the need of a blotter page.

• To avoid any "Uh Oh's" and the associated disappointment, Marker and Gel Pen users are **STRONGLY ENCOURAGED** to **USE A BLOTTER SHEET** behind the drawing to avoid any possibility of bleed through to the next page. Several blank blotter and color testing pages are provided at the end of this book.

• Most **IMPORTANT** of all: Relax, have fun, stand-up and stretch often, and remember that sometimes the most beautiful things come from what we think at first are mistakes, but which turn out to be art's way of working magic!

This Book Belongs

To

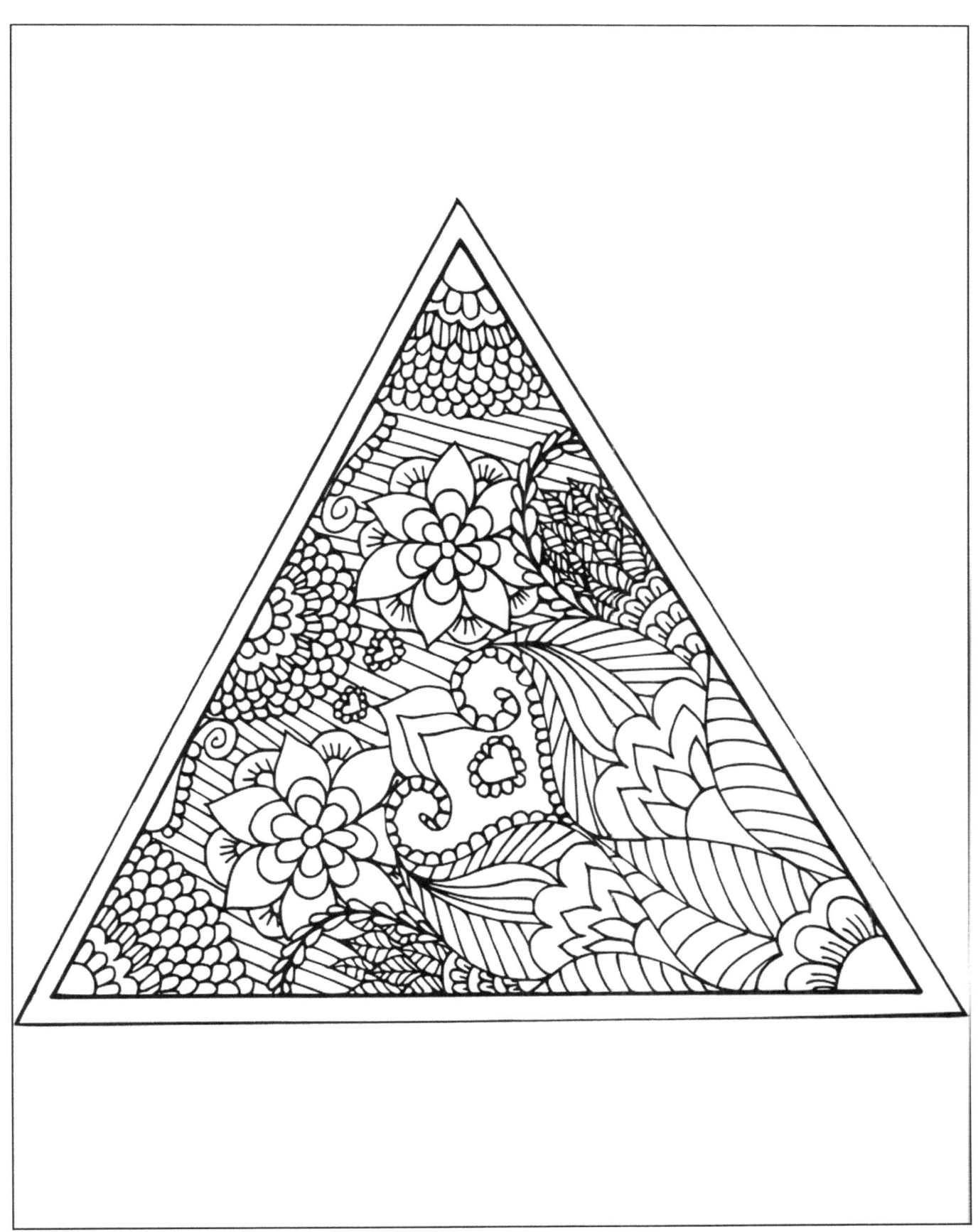

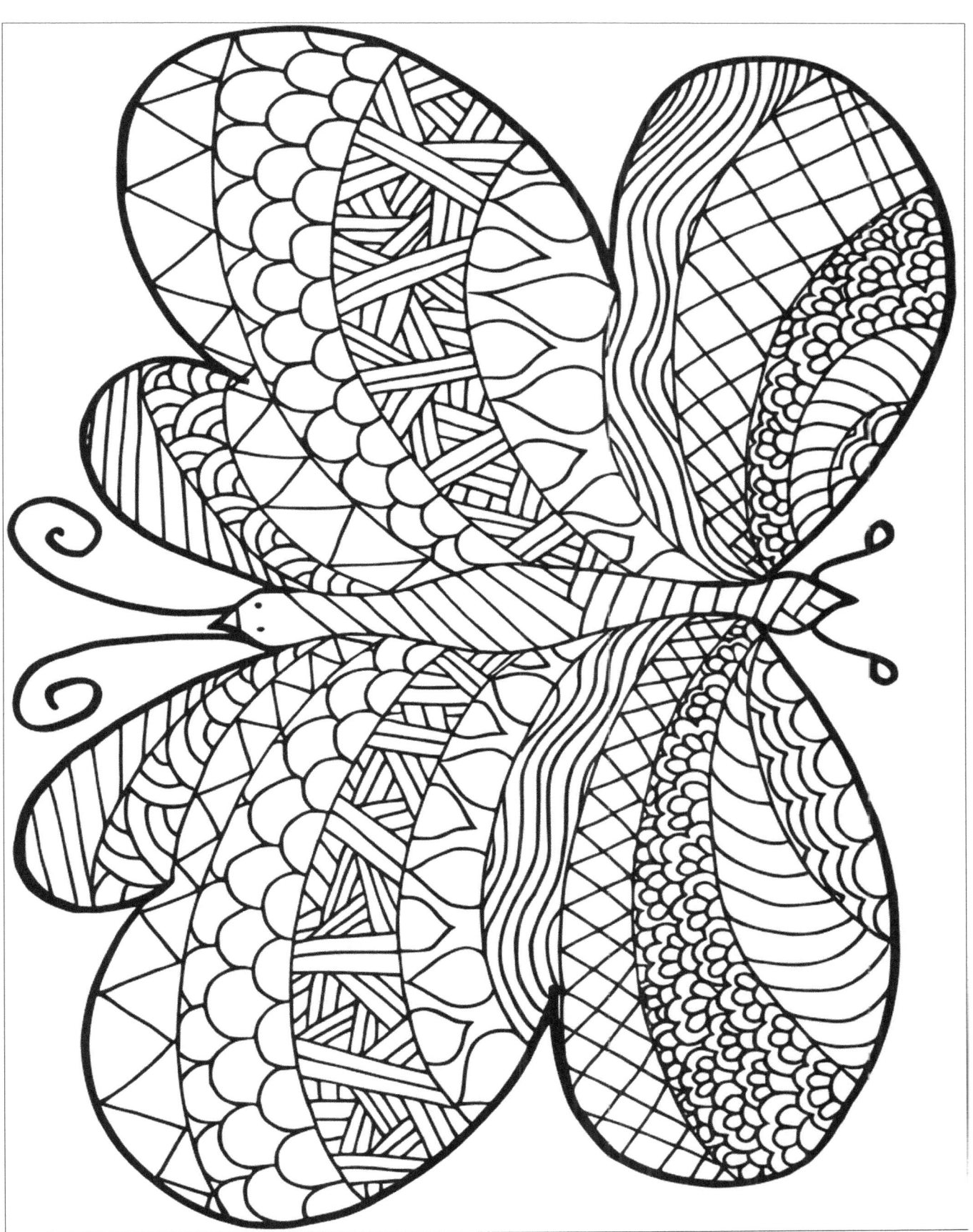

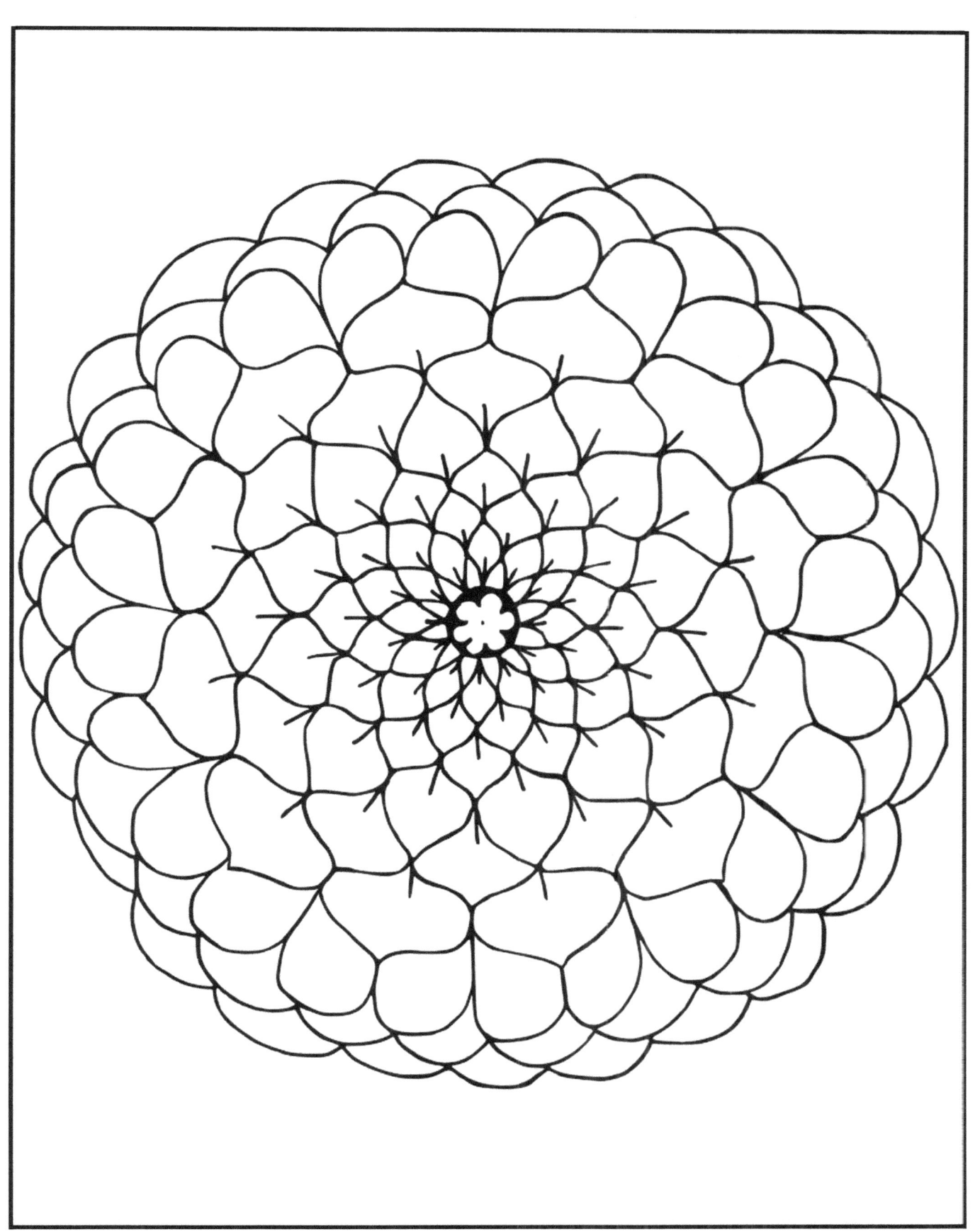

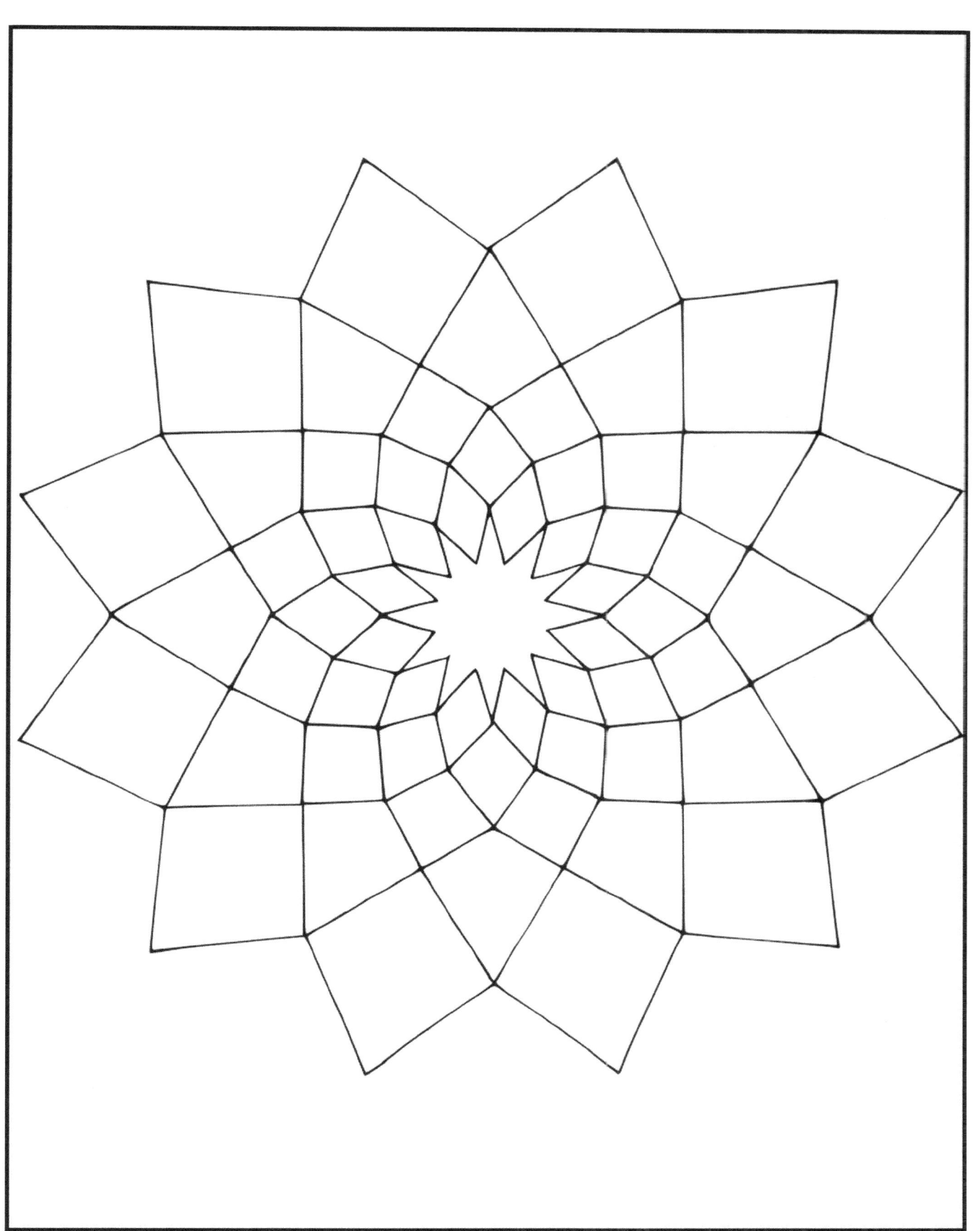

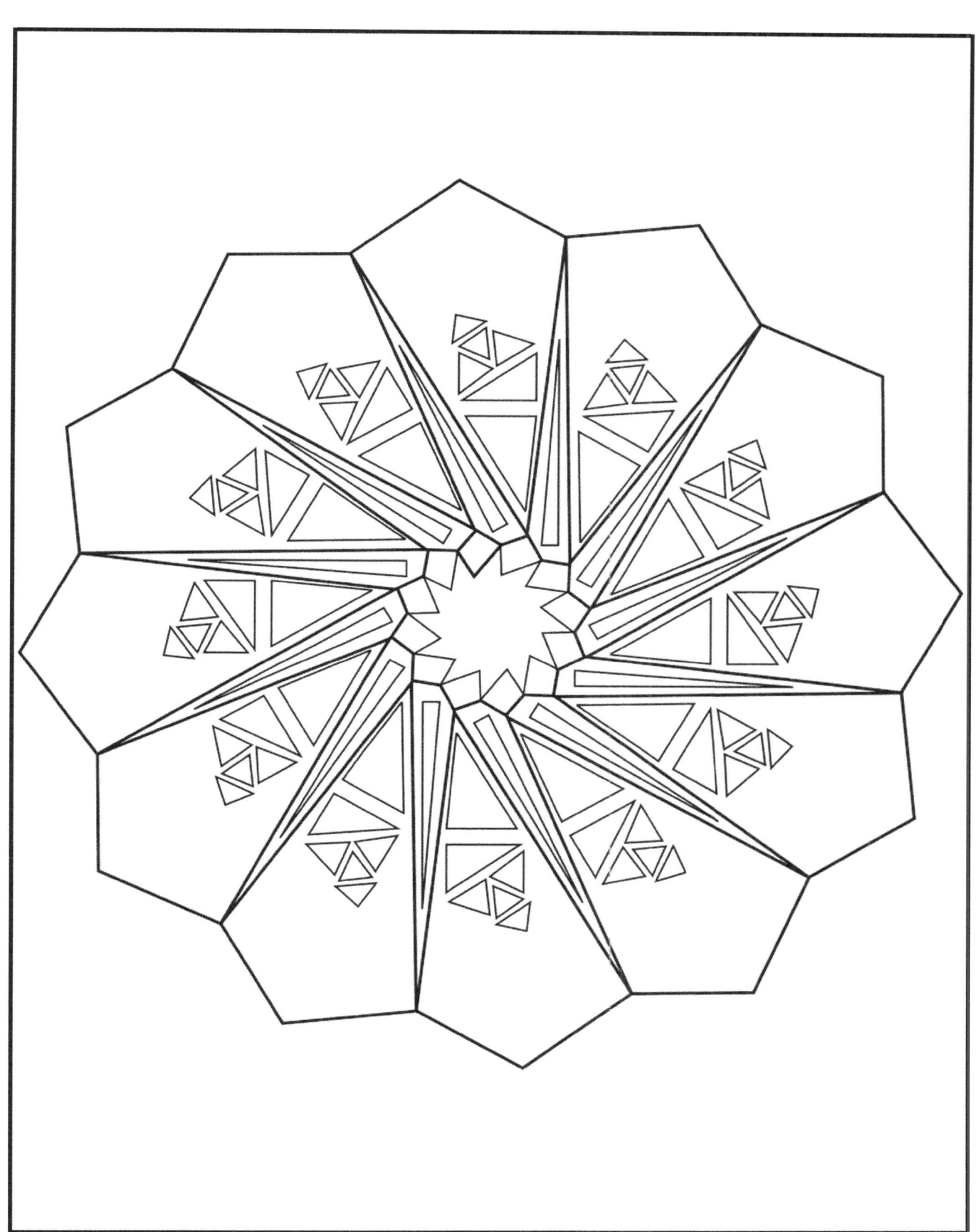

Color Testing Paper

Color Testing Paper